JFK

HISTORY IN AN HOUR

Also in the *History in an Hour* series

JFK

History in an Hour

SINEAD FITZGIBBON

WILLIAM
COLLINS

William Collins
An imprint of HarperCollins*Publishers* Ltd
77–85 Fulham Palace Road
Hammersmith, London W6 8JB
www.harpercollins.co.uk

Visit the History in an Hour website:
www.historyinanhour.com

Published by William Collins in 2013

First published as an eBook by Harper*Press* in 2012

Copyright © Sinead Fitzgibbon 2012
Series editor: Rupert Colley
HISTORY IN AN HOUR ® is a registered trademark of
HarperCollins*Publishers* Limited

1

Sinead Fitzgibbon asserts the moral right to
be identified as the author of this work

A catalogue record for this book
is available from the British Library

ISBN 978-0-00-753653-5

Find out more about HarperCollins and the environment at
www.harpercollins.co.uk/green

Contents

Introduction

Few in political history have enjoyed the kind of instant recognition afforded to John Fitzgerald Kennedy, America's 35th President. Known simply as JFK, Kennedy's good looks and easy charm were potently deployed through the newly influential medium of television. This meant that his journey to the White House captured the imagination of millions of people, both domestically and internationally.

For many, Kennedy's inauguration heralded a bright new dawn for US politics. At just forty-three, he was the youngest man ever to be elected President; he was also the first Roman Catholic. With youth, charisma and widespread popularity on his side, the future seemed bright.

Unfortunately, he was denied the chance to live up to his early promise. Barely one thousand days into his presidency, which had been marred by civil unrest in the segregated South and the threat of nuclear war from the Soviet Union, Kennedy's life was curtailed by an assassin's bullet in Dallas, Texas, in 1963. The country's youngest-ever elected president thus became the youngest to die – thereby immortalizing JFK as a tragic hero.

However, since his death, details have emerged of a private life at odds with his public persona. Rumours of serial adultery, hidden health problems, a secret marriage, and even drug addictions have since blurred his once pristine image.

This, in an hour, is the history of JFK.

From the Old World to the New

By the mid-twentieth-century, the Kennedy family were among the richest and most powerful in America. Just three generations previously, JFK's paternal and maternal ancestors had endured lives of poverty in famine-stricken Ireland. Such was their deprivation that both of his great-grandfathers – Thomas Fitzgerald and Patrick Kennedy – were forced to abandon their impoverished country in search of a new and better life in the US State of Massachusetts.

In their adoptive country, both families enjoyed success in business and eventually became involved in politics. Thomas Fitzgerald's son – John Francis Fitzgerald, known as 'Honey Fitz' – was a member of both the US House of Representatives and the Massachusetts Senate, in addition to serving two terms as Boston's first Irish–Catholic mayor. After making his fortune from whiskey importation and a successful foray into banking,

Patrick Kennedy's only son, PJ, also turned his mind to a career in public service. PJ Kennedy would eventually serve five years in the Massachusetts House of Representatives, as well as six years in the State Senate.

On 7 October 1914, after a seven-year courtship, Honey Fitz's eldest daughter, Rose, married PJ Kennedy's eldest son, Joseph, thus merging these two influential Irish–American clans.

Early Life

John Fitzgerald Kennedy
Born Brookline, Mass. (83 Beals Street) May 29, 1917

With these few simple words, handwritten on a notecard, Rose Kennedy recorded the birth of her second son – a handsome blue-eyed boy who, although named after his maternal grandfather, would become known as 'Jack'.

The family's fortunes had continued to improve in the three years since the Fitzgerald–Kennedy marriage. By the time of Jack's birth, they lived a comfortable upper-middle-class life in the Boston suburb of Brookline. Over the years, Joe would successfully try his hand at a number of businesses, including stock market speculation, movie producing, and liquor importation. By 1927, the family had moved to the exclusive suburb of Riverdale, New York.

Despite the privileged circumstances of his birth, Jack was unlucky in his health. A sickly child, he suffered from numerous childhood illnesses, including whooping cough, chicken pox, and measles. And then, three months shy of his third birthday, Jack contracted a virulent strain of scarlet fever – a potentially deadly disease in these days prior to the discovery of penicillin. For a time, it appeared that Jack would succumb to the illness, but after a month in hospital, he began to recover. He would continue to struggle with ill-health for the rest of his life.

Despite spending much of his childhood confined to a hospital bed or cooped up in a sanatorium, Jack did manage to attend school. In 1931, after a brief and unhappy stint at the Catholic Canterbury High School, the fourteen-year-old boy enrolled at Choate, an exclusive Episcopalian boarding school in Connecticut.

At Choate, Jack excelled socially and, to a lesser extent, academically. He made friends easily, and despite being a disruptive influence in class, scored relatively well in tests. His schoolmasters, however, were exasperated by his unwillingness to take instruction, resulting in his near expulsion on at least one occasion.

Before leaving Choate in 1935 (graduating 65th out of his class of 110), Jack was interviewed by a school psychologist about his obstreperous behaviour. During this conversation, the seventeen-year-old Jack revealed, perhaps inadvertently, feelings of inadequacy: 'If my brother were not so efficient, it would be easier for me to be efficient', he said, 'he does it much better than I do.'

The brother referred to here is Joseph Junior, Jack's elder brother. Sharing his father's outlook and disposition, and being more robust than his sibling, Joe Jr had always been Joe Sr's favoured son, thus bearing the weight of his family's considerable expectations. In fact, not long after Joe Jr's birth, Honey

Fitz had declared (only slightly facetiously) that his parents had 'already decided that he is going to Harvard, where he will play on the football and baseball teams and incidentally take all the scholastic honours. Then he is going to be a captain of industry until it's time for him to be President for two or three terms. Further than that has not been decided.'

Perhaps due to the poor state of his health, no such plans were made for Jack. And so, although the Kennedy clan would eventually swell to nine children, Joe Jr was the sibling with whom Jack felt he had to compete – indeed, this atmosphere of fraternal competitiveness would ultimately dictate much of the direction of Jack's entire life.

The Harvard Years

Upon leaving Choate, Jack embarked on the first of numerous European visits in his lifetime. Travelling with his father, he set sail for England to study for a year at the London School of Economics (LSE). By now, Joe Sr's wealth had increased dramatically, and although rumours persisted that not all the Kennedy fortune had been acquired entirely legitimately, the family's social standing and influence had nonetheless improved significantly. A sojourn at the LSE seemed like an ideal way to continue the young man's cultivation.

However, in late July, not long after arriving, Jack fell seriously ill, and despite a lengthy hospital stay and numerous tests, a definitive diagnosis was not possible. He returned to the United States in mid-October when his mystery illness began to improve.

Emerging from the shadows of his father and brother (both of whom attended Harvard), Jack chose to study at Princeton University. His Princeton career did not last long though – his recurring, and as yet undiagnosed illness relapsed just a month into his studies forcing him to withdraw.

In 1936, after much cajoling from his father, Jack agreed to apply to Harvard. True enough, his father's advice proved sound when, just three days after submitting his application, he received a notice of acceptance from the alma mater of so many family members. And so, despite significant resistance on his part, and like so many other aspects of John Fitzgerald Kennedy's life, he found himself following a path which had been charted by his domineering father.

At Harvard, where he studied for a Bachelor of Science in International Affairs, Jack's academic record was uninspiring. Despite displaying a keen intelligence, his grades were far from stellar. Although he loved competitive sport, his less-than-robust physicality meant that he never matched his older brother's achievements on the football field. By all accounts, Jack showed little interest in campus politics, preferring instead to leave all such politicking to Joe Jr, who was two years ahead of him. Indeed, it seems Jack only came into his own in his final two years – a period which coincided rather tellingly, with his brother's graduation. During this time, he became more involved in his studies and was increasingly fascinated by international affairs.

Taking a semester off from his studies, Jack travelled to Europe during the winter of 1938 and the spring and summer of 1939. By now, Joe Sr had himself become involved in politics, being appointed as Ambassador to Great Britain by President Roosevelt in December 1937 – a position which provided Jack with a unique vantage point from which to view the unfolding European crisis, and the increasing aggression of Nazi Germany. In the event, Jack was present in the visitor's gallery of the House of Commons when Prime Minister Neville Chamberlain took to the floor to explain his Government's decision to declare war on Germany.

The main result of Jack's European vacations was his final year thesis, which examined Britain's policy of Appeasement in the face of Nazi aggression. This 148-page document, entitled *Appeasement in Munich,* was his most serious academic effort. Its objective was not to apportion blame for the failure of Appeasement, but rather to understand why Britain had found itself, once again, on the verge of war.

Meanwhile, debate raged at home about the relative merits of a possible US intervention in the worsening European conflict. Indeed, so topical was this issue, *Appeasement in Munich* was published as a book, called *Why England Slept*, in 1940. The publication posted impressive sales figures, selling more than 80,000 copies in the US and the UK. The success of his first foray into authorship highlighted, not for the last time, Jack's ability to tap into the zeitgeist. And so, despite a lacklustre start to his college career, his profile was in the ascendancy by the time he graduated in 1940.

War Service

The interventionist debate was rendered immaterial following the Japanese attack on Pearl Harbour on 7 December 1941 – an act of aggression which forced the US to declare war on Japan the following day.

Despite its relatively late entry into World War Two, the US was not unprepared for combat. Conscription had been re-introduced in September 1940 and Jack Kennedy was among the first to be called up for the draft. Unlike his father, who had avoided enlisting during World War One, the younger Kennedy was keen to play his part. Whether this eagerness to serve was due to a genuine sense of patriotic duty or competitiveness with his older brother, who had volunteered for the navy, is debatable. Regardless, he was refused admission to both the army and navy after failing medical examinations and left bitterly disappointed.

Characteristically, the twenty-three-year-old refused to yield to this latest health-related setback and lobbied his father to intervene. Such was Joe Sr's political influence that, in less than a month, his second son somehow managed to recover from his illness to be pronounced 'physically qualified for appointment' by a committee of medical examiners. In October 1941, Kennedy entered the United States Navy as a junior officer.

A brief stint in the Foreign Intelligence Branch of the Office of Naval Intelligence was brought to an abrupt end in early 1942 when Kennedy was transferred from Washington DC to Charleston Navy Yard in South Carolina. In March, his recurrent back pain became intolerable, forcing him to seek medical help from a number of specialists, none of whom could agree on a diagnosis. Disheartened by his persistent ailments and upset by the recent breakdown of his romantic relationship with a beautiful Danish reporter named Inga Arvad – at the time suspected of being a Nazi spy – Jack requested a deployment to sea.

Following an intensive sixty-day training course, he applied for the position of commander of a torpedo boat (also known as a Patrol Torpedo or PT), which were being used to attack Japanese ships in the Pacific. His back problems were initially expected to work against him, but again, some manoeuvrings by his father Joe Sr and his grandfather, Honey Fitz, navigated the problem. By March 1943, Lt Kennedy was posted to the Solomon Islands as commander of PT-109.

Behind Enemy Lines

Jack had never made any secret of his desire for front-line combat. This deployment to one of the central battlegrounds in the fierce fight for dominance in the Pacific would provide it.

On the night of 2 August PT-109 was on a routine patrol when it was rammed by a huge Japanese destroyer. Given the size differential, the small PT boat didn't stand a chance – it was virtually sawn in half by the enemy ship, before bursting into flames. Lt Kennedy was at the helm at the time of collision, trying in vain to steer clear of the oncoming destroyer, and was flung violently against the wall by the force of the impact, badly injuring his already weak back.

He, however, was one of the lucky ones – of the twelve other crewmen on board, two lost their lives instantly. The remaining ten, along with Kennedy, were forced to abandon ship, plunged into the sea and had to cling to debris in order to remain afloat. Having sustained severe burns to his hands and face, one crewman, Patrick McMahon, struggled to reach the piece of floating hull which his comrades were using as a lifebuoy; Kennedy swam to the wounded man's rescue and pulled him to safety.

After nine hours in the water, the men reached a cluster of small islands which were situated a few miles away from the collision site, behind enemy lines. Ignoring his own back injury, Jack had pulled McMahon the whole way by clamping a strap of his life jacket between his teeth, while the wounded man floated on his back.

Having been discovered by natives who were sympathetic to their plight (and who may, in fact, have been Allied scouts), Jack arranged for a coconut shell to be smuggled to the nearest US naval base. The shell had inscribed the following message:

NAURO ISL...COMMANDER...NATIVE KNOWS POS'IT...HE CAN PILOT...11 ALIVE...NEED SMALL BOAT...KENNEDY.

The following morning, eight islanders arrived with food and water. They then concealed Kennedy under palm fronds and delivered him to Gamu, a nearby island where the local Allied coastwatcher could be found. From there, and with the help of the coastwatcher, Kennedy orchestrated the rescue of the rest of the crew, which was carried out under cover of darkness in the small hours of 8 August. The operation was a success. After six long days, the ordeal was over.

Kennedy's remarkable resourcefulness saved not only his own life but also the lives of his surviving ten crewmen. When news of his exploits reached US shores, he was lauded as a hero. In recognition of his bravery and leadership, he was awarded the Navy and Marine Corps Medal in June 1944, while the injuries to his back earned him the Purple Heart Medal.

There was, however, another memento which Jack seemed to value more than anything else. Upon returning home, he had the life-saving coconut shell mounted on a wooden base and enshrined in a plastic dome. The resulting paper-weight remained in his possession for the rest of his life, and when he became president, it took pride of place on his desk in the Oval Office.

Triumph to Tragedy

In keeping with their sibling rivalry, Joe Jr, in a letter dated August 10, voiced his obvious scepticism. 'Where the hell were you when the destroyer hove into sight', Joe Jr asked, 'and exactly what were your moves, and where the hell was your radar?' Suspecting that his brother was in some way culpable for the accident, Joe Jr became more intent than ever on outdoing his brother's achievements. Joe Jr's cynicism was also echoed in other quarters, with some suggesting that Kennedy could not have being paying attention to have allowed a destroyer to get so close. All such criticism was, however, drowned out by those extolling his courage and ingenuity during the subsequent rescue.

Having gained his wings in 1942, Joe Jr had spent much of the war in England, flying around the coastline on anti-submarine patrols. His attitude became increasingly reckless. Refusing to return home after flying thirty missions (which was his entitlement), Joe

Jr chose instead to stay on, volunteering for ever more dangerous assignments – until finally his luck ran out.

On 12 August 1944, Lt Joseph Kennedy and his co-pilot, Lt Wilford John Willy, took to the air in a B-24 Liberator packed with 22,000lbs of dynamite, the maximum amount of explosives that could be carried by a plane at the time. Their target, on the Belgian coast, was the launching site of the German V-1 flying bombs (Doodlebugs), which had been bombarding London since June. Their plan was to fly to 2,000 feet, activate the remote control system, arm explosives, and parachute from the aircraft. Joe Jr, no doubt aware that a number of previous attempts at such an attack had ended disastrously, reportedly asked a friend to 'tell my Dad that I love him very much', should he not come back.

Joe Jr didn't come back. The explosives ignited not long after take-off, engulfing the plane in a ball of fire in the skies over South East England. Joe Jr's body, and that of his co-pilot, were never recovered.

The death of the eldest son left the Kennedys shaken. Aside from his grief, Jack was also greatly upset by the realization that his brother had now become idealized in his father's eyes and thus a figure of impossibly high comparison. 'I'm shadowboxing', he said, 'in a match the shadow is always going to win.'

Passing the Baton

No longer able to hide the extent of his medical problems – which, by this stage, ranged from stomach problems, intestinal problems including spastic colitis, incessant back pain, weight loss, and jaundicing of the skin – Kennedy was discharged from the Navy on medical grounds in March 1945.

He now tried his hand at journalism, writing a number of articles as he recuperated from back surgery. One particular piece, in which he called on the US to avoid entering an arms race with the Soviet Union, brought him to the attention of the newspaper magnate, Randolph Hearst. As soon as he regained his strength, Hearst despatched the 28-year-old to San Francisco to cover the United Nations conference. In all, he wrote seventeen short pieces – often highlighting the growing tensions between the West and the USSR – which were published in the *Chicago Herald-American*. But instead of establishing a journalistic career, Kennedy's experience at the UN conference whetted his appetite for post-war international politics.

But if he harboured any doubts about his future direction, his father soon dispelled them. It was no secret that Joe Sr had long held ambitious plans to establish his family as a political force, and now, in the stead of his favoured eldest son, he encouraged Jack to fulfil these hopes.

But it would not be easy. 'He [Joe Jr] was altogether different from Jack,' the Kennedy patriarch once said. '[Joe Jr was] more dynamic, more sociable, more easy-going. Jack [...] was rather shy, withdrawn and quiet. His mother and I couldn't picture him as a politician.' Nevertheless, Joe Sr persevered, telling a reporter in 1957:

> I got Jack into politics. I was the one. I told him Joe was dead and that it was therefore his responsibility to run for Congress. He didn't want to do it. He felt he didn't have the ability and he still feels that way. But I told him he had to do it.

For his part, Jack likened the onslaught from his father in loaded terms. 'It was like being drafted', he said, 'my father wanted his eldest son in politics. "Wanted" isn't the right word. He demanded it.' Initially, he rebelled instinctively and resisted the pressure. 'Dad is ready right now,' he said to a friend, 'and can't understand why Johnny boy isn't all engines ahead full.'

Unable to deny his father, 'Johnny boy' relented, and in April 1946, declared his candidacy for the Democratic Party's nomination to run for the 11th Congressional District of Massachusetts seat in the House of Representatives. If successful in winning his party's backing, Jack would go head-to-head against the Republican Party's candidate in the general election on 5 November 1946. He had at last entered the political arena.

Political Beginnings

For a man who would one day enjoy widespread popularity as President of the United States, the success of John Fitzgerald Kennedy's first sortie into campaign politics was far from assured. The 11th Congressional District of Massachusetts, being a largely working-class area, was not the most familiar arena for the privileged progeny of a multi-millionaire businessman. In addition, Kennedy's complete lack of experience in local politics made matters more difficult.

As is always the case in the political arena, his rivals were only too willing to denigrate the newcomer. 'This candidate has never held public office', declared one of his nine opponents, 'he is registered at the Hotel Bellevue in Boston, and I daresay he has never slept there. He comes from New York. His father is a resident of Florida. This candidate [...] knows nothing about the problems of its people.'

Moreover, it wasn't just his political adversaries who were vocal in their detraction of his candidacy – some of the local newspapers also took umbrage this interloper. The *East-Boston Leader*, for example, published this damagingly satirical advert, lampooning Jack's candidature: 'Congress seat for sale – No experience necessary – Applicant must live in New York or Florida – Only millionaires need apply.'

However, Jack's combined Fitzgerald–Kennedy name helped to counter this negative press in some quarters, as both his grandfathers were well-liked in the Massachusetts State political community. Kennedy also emphasized his war-hero reputation and positioned himself as a committed advocate of war veterans.

His campaign also tapped into the issues of most concern to the constituents of the 11th District. Recognizing that his family's wealth alienated him from a significant part of the blue-collar electorate, Kennedy worked to bridge this gap by promising more jobs, higher wages, improved Social Security and better housing.

While Jack was busy on the campaign trail promising to raise the minimum wage to 65 cents an hour, Joe Sr was, somewhat ironically, equally busy behind the scenes, pumping vast amounts of cash into his son's election bid. It is estimated that as much as $300,000 of Kennedy money changed hands in the run up to the election, much of it as underhand cash payments to oil the creaky cogs of the local political machine.

Nevertheless, much of the credit for the success of his campaign lay with Kennedy himself. Much to his surprise, and indeed that of his father, the young Kennedy greatly enjoyed his time out on the hustings. He was unfazed by his opponents' attacks on his character – indeed, if anything, the rough and tumble of campaign politics appealed to the competitive side of his nature. Overcoming his innate shyness, he grew more confident with every speech he gave. Soon, Just as it had done at school and in the navy, his quiet natural charisma earned him many admirers.

This broadening fan-base supported him at the ballot boxes. He gained 40.5 per cent of the votes, and won the Democratic Party's nomination, after which his victory over the Republican candidate was a matter of course. In a State populated predominantly by Democrats, the twenty-nine-year-old defeated his main rival 69,093 votes to 26,007 in the General Election on 5 November 1946.

The journey to the White House had begun.

Onwards and Upwards

Kennedy's maiden term in office as a Congressman was beset with frustrations. In 1947, the Republican Party enjoyed a majority in the House of Representatives, which meant that Democrat members were often out-numbered in critical votes. Hamstrung, it was extremely difficult for a young and inexperienced Democrat like Kennedy to make any great impression during his first term in Washington. Nevertheless, his popularity did not wane, and he was re-elected for two further two-year terms, in 1948 and 1950.

By the end of his third Congressional term in 1952, Kennedy decided to set his sights on the Senate. The House of Representatives had never been more than a stepping stone and he had already considered and rejected the possibility of running for the job of Massachusetts State Governor.

It was announced that he would be challenging the Republican incumbent, Henry Cabot Lodge Jr, for his seat in the Upper House in April. The decision was a brave one – Lodge was firmly estab-lished in the position of State Senator for Massachusetts, while at a national level, the Republican Party's candidate, Dwight Eisenhower, was ahead in the concurrent Presidential race.

Once again, the Kennedy family rallied. As in the 1946 campaign, Joe Sr invested huge sums of money to bankroll his son's ambitious campaign. Consequently, despite hailing from a wealthy family himself, Henry Cabot Lodge was, in Eisenhower's words, 'simply overwhelmed by money.'

Funding gap aside, it became obvious as the campaign progressed that very little separated the two candidates. From a policy point of view, both held similar views on domestic and international affairs, despite being on opposite sides of the party divide. And when it came to the burning issue of the day – Communism – both men tried to out-do each other in proving their commitment to an anti-Communist agenda.

Thus, with Kennedy struggling to differentiate himself ideologi-cally from his rival, it was decided, midway through the campaign, to deploy the biggest (and, as it proved, most effective) weapon in the Kennedy family arsenal – Jack's younger brother, Robert. Drafted in as campaign manager, Robert (known as Bobby), aban-doned his career as an attorney with the Department of Justice – somewhat reluctantly at first – to devote his considerable energies to the task of getting his brother elected to the Senate.

Often working up to eighteen hours a day, Bobby devised and implemented a highly effective campaign strategy. Thanks to his organizational skills, the Kennedy canvassers succeeded in infil-trating practically every highway, byway and backwater of the State of Massachusetts – with the result that, by the time the polls opened on 5 November, there could hardly have been a voter in the entire State who was not acquainted with the name and face of John Fitzgerald Kennedy.

In the end, this name-recognition – bought by Joe's money and hammered home by Bobby's thorough campaign strategies – helped Kennedy over the line. In a time when Republicans were winning landslide victories across the country, he bucked the trend and won by 51.5 per cent to 48.5 per cent. Winning just 70,000 more votes than his opponent, out of approximately 2.3 million votes cast, Kennedy narrowly dethroned Lodge.

The forward momentum of the powerful Kennedy machine, it seemed, was unstoppable.

A Medical Breakthrough

As it transpired, Kennedy had a significant weakness, and had his political opponents discovered this, it would have proved fatal for his burgeoning career.

In 1947, after years of inconclusive tests, his doctors had finally hit upon an explanation for the dizzying array of illnesses which had seen him hospitalized almost forty times throughout his life – and which, it is rumoured, caused him to receive the Last Rites no less than three times. Kennedy suffered from Addison's Disease.

Addison's is a rare disorder characterized by underactive adrenal glands and a deficiency of a hormone known as adrenocortical. A progressive and incurable illness, it dramatically decreases the life expectancy of the sufferer. But, luckily for Kennedy, a scientific breakthrough in the late 1940s saw the introduction of a synthetic compound to replace the deficient hormone, meaning that the disease was now treatable.

Once his diagnosis was confirmed, Jack was prescribed a high (and potentially dangerous) dose of corticosteroid, which he would take daily for the rest of his life. While the disease was far from cured, his ever-worsening symptoms were at least brought temporarily under control, allowing him to keep his illness controlled and concealed during the arduous election campaigns of 1948, 1950, and 1952.

In fact, rumours that Jack suffered from Addison's only began to surface a decade later, during the 1960 Presidential campaign – and were advisedly denied by the Kennedy camp. The full truth about Jack's affliction only emerged after the election, by which time it no longer mattered as Kennedy was safely installed in the White House as President of the United States.

When Jack Met Jackie

In an echo of his burgeoning political career, Kennedy's widespread popularity had inevitably spilled over into his private life. While he had never been short of admirers, his public profile only increased his eligibility. Despite entertaining a host of girlfriends, he showed little inclination to bring his bachelorhood to an end by settling down with a wife.

This was, at least, how the situation was perceived in public. Privately, it may have been a different matter entirely. For the past sixty years, rumours have persisted that in 1947 Jack secretly married a wealthy Episcopalian divorcee named Durie Malcolm. No definitive evidence has ever emerged, and so these rumours – along with reports that, upon hearing of the alleged nuptials, a furious Joe Sr arranged for the official records to be expunged – remain unproven.

Nevertheless, there is no secret about the fact that, by the early

1950s, the Kennedy patriarch was becoming increasingly eager to see Jack safely married off to a suitable wife – one who would complement, if not enhance, his son's public profile.

The beautiful and sophisticated Jacqueline Lee Bouvier, of French, English, and Irish ancestry and the daughter of a successful Wall Street stockbroker, seemed the perfect choice. Crucially, she was from a Catholic family, had received an exemplary education, and exuded a natural elegance and charm – an ideal match, it seemed, for a man like Jack Kennedy.

Towards the end of 1951, Jackie began working as a writer and photographer for the *Washington Times-Herald* newspaper. Her weekly column, *Inquiring Camera Girl*, brought her into the sphere of Washington's political elite. The pair met briefly in late 1951 and then again in May 1952 over dinner at the home of a mutual friend. A courtship began which, despite some prevarication on Kennedy's part, culminated in a marriage proposal a year later. The nuptials took place on 12 September 1953, ten months after he was elected to the Senate – the groom was thirty-six, the bride twenty-four.

It has been suggested that Kennedy married Jackie purely to satisfy his father and advance his political career. Despite the problems that would later afflict their marriage, Jack's friend, Chuck Spalding, believed that it was, in the beginning at least, a love match:

> Jack appreciated her … He really brightened when she appeared. You could see it in his eyes; he'd follow her around the room watching to see what she'd do next. Jackie interested him, which was not true of many women.

A telegram he sent to his parents while on honeymoon certainly seems to suggest he was enamoured with his new wife: 'At last

I know the true meaning of rapture,' he said. 'Jackie is forever enshrined in my heart.' Washington's most eligible politician, it seemed, was content.

Till Death Do Us Part?

However, it was not long before the marriage became troubled. Barely a year after their lavish wedding, Jackie had grown disillusioned with her lot as a political wife, bemoaning the fact that her husband was often away on political business. Her husband had returned swiftly to his bachelor ways, often seeking out the company of pretty young girls. Indeed, his persistent adultery, often barely concealed from Jackie, would continue be a constant source of friction between the couple.

Kennedy's illnesses also put considerable strain on the marriage – in a bid to relieve his constant back pain, he underwent two potentially life-threatening spinal operations in the months following the wedding, both of which were only partially successful. The continuing chronic pain often had a detrimental effect on his mood, leaving him prone to bursts of anger.

There were, however, some positives to emerge from this fraught time. While he was recuperating from his operations, Jackie encouraged her husband to use the time wisely by writing another book. The resulting tome, *Profiles in Courage,* which examined the careers of eight prominent US Senators who had fought against the odds for causes they believed in, was published in 1956. An instant bestseller, the book went on to win the Pulitzer Prize for Biography the following year. The success of the book, however, did little to mitigate the couple's worsening relationship, which almost irreparably broke down in August 1956 when Jackie gave birth to a stillborn daughter (whom, it is believed, was to be named Arabella).

Having previously suffered an early-term miscarriage, Jackie was devastated by the loss of her child at such a late stage in her pregnancy. Her misery was further compounded by the fact her husband was reluctant to cut short a European vacation to be by her side – a fact which is said to have brought the couple close to divorce.

The arrival of a healthy daughter, Caroline, in November 1957, went some way towards healing the couple's fractured relationship, and with her husband having by now decided to run for the White House, Jackie set aside her misgivings. With her sights now firmly focused on bigger and better things – namely the role of First Lady – all talk of divorce evaporated.

A Small Setback

By the late 1950s, the extent of Kennedy's presidential ambitions had become obvious to all concerned. Indeed, the writing had been on the wall as early as 1956, when the Massachusetts Senator put himself forward for consideration as the Democratic Party's vice presidential candidate, to run alongside presidential hopeful, Adlai Stevenson.

On that occasion, Kennedy narrowly lost out to Senator Estes Kefauver of Tennessee. In the end, the Stevenson–Kefauver ticket was defeated by a large margin when the incumbent, President Eisenhower, secured a second term. Avoiding association with such a defeat may have even benefitted Kennedy.

With his White House hopes pushed onto the back-burner for the next four years, Kennedy re-focused his attentions on his role in the Senate. His achievements in the United States Senate had been limited, due to the enforced absences caused by his back surgeries. He had also suffered serious reputational damage in 1954 as a result of his abstention from a Senate vote to condemn Senator Joseph McCarthy's excessive anti-Communist investigations, despite his stated opposition to them.

Many have questioned why Kennedy refused to display the courage of his convictions in the McCarthy affair. Why did he take such an uncharacteristic political risk by failing to take a stand on this much-publicized issue? The answer lay, once again, in his suffocating family ties. His father had been a vocal McCarthy supporter and, more importantly, his brother, Bobby was working for McCarthy at the time. He later recalled:

> I was caught in a bad situation. My brother was working for Joe. [...] And how the hell could I get up there and denounce Joe McCarthy when my own brother was working for him?

Despite his weak showing in the McCarthy affair, Kennedy was successful in his re-election bid in 1958. Indeed, he confounded his detractors by beating his rival by the widest margin ever recorded in Massachusetts Senate race. Fears that his back problems, which had been impossible to hide during his first term, would count against him proved unfounded. Nevertheless, he still refused to admit to the full extent of his health problems, continuing to believe that such a disclosure would damage his presidential prospects.

During his brief second term in the Senate, Kennedy did try to make amends for his McCarthy debacle by backing anti-Communist foreign policies, as well as supporting changes to labour legislation. But the progress made on these issues was soon overshadowed in January 1960 when he officially declared candidacy for President.

The Right Man for the Job?

Before Kennedy could set about convincing the country to elect him as president, he first had to win the Democratic nomination.

Encouragingly, the political winds had turned noticeably in Jack's favour in the four years that had passed since his failed attempt to gain his party's nomination for vice president. Always a firm favourite in Massachusetts, Kennedy's profile had also been raised at a national level, thanks in large part to an exhaustive speaking tour in 1957. However, side from a general uneasiness among the party at Joe Sr's continuing interference in his son's career, there were two other concerns.

Firstly, his age – at just forty-three, some thought it inappropriate – and perhaps even arrogant – that Jack should be campaigning for the presidential nomination, and suggested that a vice-presidential bid would be more fitting. The second difficulty was his Catholic faith. Never in the country's history had a Catholic been elected President (and none since). Given that America was still a predominantly Protestant country, Catholicism was viewed somewhat suspiciously in certain quarters, with some fearing a Catholic president would pander too much to the Vatican when it came to affairs of State.

Characteristically, Jack navigated the criticism with a mix of humour, steel, and political insight. He laughed off charges that his father was engaging in some less-than-savoury electioneering practices on his behalf, while doing his best to allay fears that he would be unduly influenced by the Pope. With regard to the problem of his age, Kennedy cleverly worked this to his advantage – portraying himself as an energetic, rejuvenating force in the wake of the older Eisenhower regime. Kennedy's campaign to win his Party's presidential nomination pitched him against a number of other high-profile Democrats including Adlai Stevenson and Lyndon B Johnson. The battle was hard fought with Johnson, in particular, making personal attacks on Kennedy by raising the possibility that he suffered from Addison's Disease.

The Kennedy family doctors refused to confirm the Addison's diagnosis, helping repel this attack. At the Democratic Convention in July 1960, Kennedy garnered 806 votes – 52 per cent of total ballots cast – making him an outright winner. His nearest rival, Lyndon B Johnson, won the vice-presidential nomination.

After a fractious campaign, both men now had to put their differences behind them if they were to have any hope of beating their Republican rivals in the general election – namely, the current Vice President, Richard Nixon, and Jack's old Senatorial rival, Henry Cabot Lodge Jr.

Presidential Campaign

From the outset, it was clear that this was going to be a close-run race. One particular Gallup survey, published in August, put the Republican ticket in front by 53 to 47 per cent, while other opinion polls declared that the candidates were too close to call.

As was the case in the primary, Kennedy's age and religion worked against him, likewise the mounting speculation about the state of his health. But, as before, Kennedy negotiated these accusations by flatly denying them and vociferously repudiating allegations that he harboured a Catholic-leaning agenda. 'I am not the Catholic candidate for President', he declared in September, 'I am the Democratic Party's candidate for President, who happens also to be a Catholic.'

Interestingly, for the first time in his career, Kennedy's rather colourful private life began to encroach on his public ambitions. Whisperings about his numerous affairs were growing louder by the day. Fortunately for Kennedy, such extra-marital affairs were not unique in Washington and many senior Republicans were reluctant to criticize his behaviour, fearful that their own infidelities would be exposed in the process.

Another obstacle was Jack's relative inexperience. With the country entering a recession, Kennedy struggled to convince voters that he had the wherewithal to reverse the economic downturn. In the face of escalating Cold War hostilities between America and the Soviet Union, surely Nixon – who had been vice president for the previous eight years – was better equipped to deal with these mounting international tensions than a relative newcomer?

In response, Kennedy drew attention to what he saw as the previous administration's poor record on these issues. He highlighted the fact that the domestic economy had faltered in 1957 and 1958, offsetting the gains of the first half of the decade. From a foreign policy standpoint, the Kennedy camp seized on an issue that had they had first used to their advantage in the 1958 Senate campaign – the perceived dominance of the Soviet Union over America in the race to produce nuclear arms.

Having been previously misled by incorrect intelligence, Kennedy erroneously claimed that defence cuts introduced by the Eisenhower–Nixon administration had allowed the USSR to overtake America's nuclear capability. Although Kennedy discovered as early as July 1960 that this perceived 'missile gap' may not in fact exist – and indeed, if it did exist, it was the United States who had the advantage – he continued to use the topic to undermine his opponent throughout the Presidential campaign.

Another factor exploited by the Kennedy campaign, once again masterminded by Bobby, was the increasingly influential medium of television. Recognizing its growing influence over the American public, Kennedy challenged Nixon to participate in an unprecedented challenge: four televised debates in the run-up to election day.

Kennedy made every effort to ensure his performance would be flawless, rehearsing his speeches, and preparing answers to any number of possible questions. Before the first debate, he went so far as to meet with the director to discuss camera angles and set lighting, with the result that he came across on-screen as more relaxed, confident, vigorous, and personable than his dour-faced rival.

By all accounts, Jack greatly benefitted from these TV debates. Post-broadcast opinion polls suggested that the majority of viewers thought Kennedy to be the clear winner – but interestingly, radio listeners disagreed, believing the victory had been Nixon's, a fact which underlines the importance of image to the Kennedy campaign.

But for all this, Kennedy struggled to close the gap with Nixon. The final Gallup survey, three days before the country went to the polls, put Nixon ahead by about 1 per cent, at 50.5 to Kennedy's 49.5 per cent. In the end, the election, on 8 November 1960, was one of the most close-run in US history – so close, in fact, that the winner was not declared until noon the following day.

Thanks in large part to Kennedy's support for Martin Luther King following the latter's arrest during a Civil Rights demonstration in Atlanta, Georgia, there was a strong turnout among the African–American community – a fact which ultimately helped Kennedy over the line. In the end, he won by a margin of just 118,550 out of almost 69 million votes cast. At last, Joe Sr's ambition had been realized – a Kennedy had finally made it to the White House.

The Birth of Camelot

On 20 January 1961, despite deep snow and plunging temperatures, as many as 20,000 people converged on Capitol Hill in Washington, all eager to bear witness to history in the making – the inauguration of the 35th President of the Unites States.

To all those huddled against the biting cold, and many millions besides, John Fitzgerald Kennedy represented all that was new and exciting about their country. JFK and Jackie – who had given birth to the couple's first son, John Jr, just two months previously – brought a youthful glamour, refinement, and culture to a White House that had become dull under the grandfatherly President Eisenhower. So strong was this mythic sense of national well-being that his time in office would later become known as the American Camelot.

Indeed, with this enormous weight of expectation bearing down heavily on his shoulders, it would have been understandable if

Kennedy had faltered on this, the most important day of his life. But instead, after solemnly swearing the Oath of Office, he stepped up to the podium and delivered one of the most inspiring speeches in US political history.

Co-written with his long-time collaborator, Ted Sorensen, Kennedy's inaugural address, delivered in his trademark Bostonian drawl, was a masterpiece in soaring rhetoric:

> Let the word go forth from this time and place, to friend and foe alike, that the torch has been passed to a new generation of Americans […] Let every nation know […]that we shall pay any price, bear any burden, meet any hardship, support any friend, oppose any foe, in order to assure the survival and the success of liberty.

But amid the optimism and ceremony on that bitter cold January day in 1961, neither Kennedy nor the US people could have known just how soon these lofty ideals would be put to the test.

The Bay of Pigs

One of Kennedy's first acts as President was the establishment of the Peace Corps, which came into existence on 1 March 1960. An unarmed volunteer organization tasked with bringing aid to second and third world countries, this admirable undertaking was widely interpreted as a signal of Kennedy's willingness to effect change by non-violent means, despite the escalating tensions of the Cold War. Unfortunately, whatever peaceable intentions the President had contemplated were compromised by the increasing problem of Cuba.

Despite its relative small size, the archipelago of islands that make up Cuba had long been a cause of concern for successive US administrations. The uncomfortable proximity of this politically volatile island nation to the United States meant any political unrest in Cuba constituted a credible threat to US national security – a danger which greatly intensified following Fidel Castro's rise to power in 1959.

The military coup which brought Castro to power coincided with a particularly dangerous time in the Cold War. The United States and the Soviet Union were engaged in a frantic nuclear arms race, while the Soviet Premier, Nikita Khrushchev, was engaging in increasingly antagonistic anti-US rhetoric. It is hardly surprising then, that the United States was not prepared to stand by while Castro – himself often espousing anti-US sentiments – established a Communist totalitarian regime just ninety miles south of the coast of Florida, which could easily be used as a Soviet outpost from which to launch an attack.

With this being so, in March 1960 President Eisenhower had authorized a covert operation by the CIA to recruit a small army of Cuban exiles who would invade their homeland and, it was hoped, bring an end to the Castro dictatorship and restore the country to democracy.

Throughout 1960, plans for what became known as *Operation Zapata* progressed. From April, the CIA recruited a motley crew of participants from the ranks of disaffected Cuban migrants in Miami, and soon training grounds were established in Florida, Panama and Guatemala. In August, a budget of $13 million was allocated to the mission, and by the time Eisenhower relinquished the presidency to Kennedy in early 1961, the Cuban invasion was almost a *fait accompli.* In fact, plans for the mission were so far advanced that Kennedy felt compelled to go along with them, despite harbouring deep reservations about the operation's chances for success.

Kennedy was right to be worried. When the invasion was launched on 17 April 1961, it was an unmitigated disaster. Cuban and Soviet intelligence had got wind of the plans, and when the army of almost 1,500 US trained revolutionaries landed in the Bay of Pigs, Castro's forces were waiting. While both sides sustained heavy losses, it didn't take long for the Cuban militia to gain the upper hand. By 19 April, all of the CIA-trained expats were either killed or captured. When news of the mission's failure and the resulting loss of life reached Kennedy at the White House, he reportedly put his head in his hands and wept.

However, if he thought things could not get any worse, he was very much mistaken.

Space Wars

The humiliating defeat of the US-sponsored mission in Cuba came at a very inopportune time for Kennedy. Now three months into his presidency, he was yet to assert his authority on the international stage. Particularly humiliating, was that the Soviets seemed to be taking the lead in the 'space race'.

Following the success of the Sputnik programme, which had seen the USSR send the first satellite into orbit in 1957, Kennedy saw that America could better her rival by being the first to launch a man into space. But it wasn't to be. On 12 April 1961, just 5 days prior to the ill-fated Cuban invasion, the Soviet cosmonaut, Lt Yuri Gagarin, became the first man to successfully orbit the earth, beating the US astronaut, Alan Shepard, by just three weeks. When Shepard did enter space on 5 May, he fell well short of Gagarin's achievements, reaching a height of only 115 miles.

So acute was American discomfiture at the success of the Soviet space programme that Kennedy felt compelled to take drastic action. On 25 May, he announced an extra $7 billion in funding to NASA, and said that, before the end of the decade, an American would walk on the moon. This bold pledge would soon be made a reality, but, cruelly, not in his lifetime.

East vs West

So far, Kennedy's inaugural year had been disastrous. It is hardly surprising then, that when he decamped to Vienna on 3 June for a two-day summit meeting with the Soviet Premier, Nikita Khrushchev, to discuss Cold War concerns, the American president was on the defensive.

One of the topics up for discussion was the contentious issue of Berlin. After World War Two, Germany had been split into two blocs – West Germany, which was further divided into three zones, occupied by France, Britain, and the United States; and East Germany, which was occupied by the USSR. In addition, Berlin, despite being situated within the Soviet zone, was similarly divided up between the four nations. And now, as Cold War hostilities intensified, the triumvirate of Western nations were growing increasingly worried that Khrushchev would deny them access to their respective enclaves in West Berlin. It was Kennedy's job to see that this didn't happen.

True to form, Khrushchev became antagonistic almost immediately, determined to take advantage of his opponent's perceived weakness. Kennedy put in a disappointing performance. His attempts to stand up to Khrushchev on disarmament, the situation in Laos, ideological differences, and other subjects were not successful. Worse, he failed to gain assurances that the Soviet Premier would not impinge on the West's interests in Berlin. Afterwards, Kennedy confessed to being out of his depth: 'He beat the hell out of me', he told a *New York Times* correspondent, 'worst thing in my life. He savaged me.'

Much speculation has followed regarding Kennedy's poor showing in Vienna. His incessant back pain, and the increasingly dangerous concoction of drugs he ingested to combat it, probably had a direct bearing on his performance. In fact, by this stage, his Addison's Disease had progressed to the point that Kennedy had become reliant on a daily shot of amphetamines, prescribed by Dr Max Jacobson (nicknamed 'Dr Feelgood' by his patients) just to get through the working day. Indeed, it is highly likely this dependence had become an addiction. Over a decade later, in 1975, Jacobson, who was by then amphetamine addict himself, had his medical licence revoked for negligently administering these drugs.

Kennedy's failure in Vienna had almost immediate repercussions. Just two months later, Khrushchev, confident that his actions would go unpunished by the 'weak' US president, persuaded East German officials to begin construction of an edifice which would become the defining image of the division between East and West – the Berlin Wall.

'Eyeball to Eyeball'

In the following months, Kennedy was criticized for his muted reaction to the Berlin Wall's construction. But, in reality, there was little he could do about it. The Wall – which had been built primarily to seal off the border between East and West, thereby stemming the flow of refugees pouring out of the Eastern Bloc – did not affect the rights of the Allied nations or interfere with their access to their enclaves in West Berlin.

Khrushchev, encouraged by his success, resolved in the summer of 1962 to implement secret plans to build a nuclear base on Cuba. In all, Khrushchev hoped to install forty medium and intermediate-range missiles on the islands, which could travel up to 2,100 miles – bringing the weapons within reach of New York and Washington DC.

But these plans did not remain secret. On 14 October, an American U-2 reconnaissance aircraft spotted and photographed the activities in Cuba. After a series of crisis meetings with his advisers, Kennedy ordered the deployment of a convoy of ships tasked with forming a ring around the Cuban islands, thereby denying the Soviets any further access to the country. The naval blockade, or 'quarantine' as it was called, was successful – the Soviet ships were stalled and Khrushchev's plans lay in ruins.

In the ensuing stand-off between the two superpowers, it seemed that the world was on the very brink of nuclear catastrophe. Tensions between the White House and the Kremlin reached crisis point. After the drubbing he received in Vienna, Kennedy was determined not to flinch this time, while Khrushchev was equally as reluctant to back down.

However, all-out war was avoided when an agreement was reached on 28 October. In exchange for US assurances that it would not invade Cuba, Khrushchev promised to dismantle the nuclear base. In a separate and secret agreement, Kennedy also promised to withdraw US missiles, which had previously been installed in Turkey.

Kennedy's actions during the thirteen-day crisis were lauded throughout the globe – he had successfully seen off the biggest nuclear threat the world had ever seen, without the loss of a single life. In the words of Dean Rusk, the US Secretary of State: 'We're eyeball to eyeball and [...] the other fellow just blinked.'

A Moral Crisis

Kennedy was allowed little time to savour his first major success on the international stage. Shortly after the curtain had fallen on the Cuban Missile Crisis another issue – one which had been simmering on the home front for some time – came close to boiling point.

Kennedy had long been a supporter of the African–American struggle against racial inequality, which was particularly prevalent in the segregated South. Indeed, in the run up to the presidential election, Kennedy had lost votes in the Southern States by coming out in support of Martin Luther King, who had been arrested at a protest in an Atlanta restaurant. Luckily, any votes lost were offset by a groundswell of support from the black community, 70 per cent of whom voted for Kennedy.

Nonetheless, the experience had left Kennedy wary of introducing any significant Civil Rights legislation during his first term in office, fearful that a backlash from the South would scupper his chances of being elected for a second term. He justified his prevarication by privately resolving to introduce reforms once a second term was secured.

But the African–American community were in no mood to wait. Civil Rights protests were becoming ever more commonplace, with many descending into violence when met with opposition from the white community. Then, in June 1963, Governor George Wallace of Alabama prevented two black students from enrolling at the State University, in contravention of a court-ordered desegregation of the institution. Kennedy, furious at Wallace's actions, was finally compelled to act.

On 11 June, Kennedy issued a presidential proclamation compelling the Alabama Governor to stand aside and allow the registration of the two students, James Alexander Hood and Vivian Malone. He also mobilized the Alabama National Guard, which was deployed to the university's campus to restore order and prevent any further violence. Finally, the President took over the prime-time 8pm slot on national television to deliver an awe-inspiring address to the American public, announcing the introduction of comprehensive Civil Rights legislation, which would eventually be passed into law in 1964:

> One hundred years of delay have passed since President Lincoln freed the slaves, yet their heirs, their grandsons, are not fully free, and this Nation [...] will not be fully free until all its citizens are free. [...] We face, therefore, a moral crisis as a country and a people.

While the majority of American people rejoiced upon hearing these words, Kennedy was worried that he had lost the support of the Southern States. As he said, 'I can kiss the south goodbye.'

Vietnam

On 7 August 1963, Jackie gave birth almost six weeks prematurely to the couple's second son, Patrick Bouvier Kennedy. Weighing a little over two kilograms, Patrick lived for only two days, before succumbing to respiratory problems. Although devastated by the loss, Kennedy had little time to grieve, as another pressing international issue demanded his attention, this time concerning Vietnam.

Since the Geneva Accord of 1954, Vietnam had been divided into two separate States: North Vietnam, controlled by the Communist, Ho Chi Minh; and the non-Communist South Vietnam, ruled by the military government of Ngo Dinh Diem. Initially, Diem enjoyed the backing of the US government, but concerns began to mount with the emergence of reports of the brutal suppression of the Buddhist population by Diem, who was Catholic. Diem's army was also struggling to quell the uprising of Vietcong guerrillas, who were supported by the Communist North Vietnamese administration. This prompted fears that, should the guerrillas succeed in defeating South Vietnamese forces, the country could very well be absorbed into Ho Chi Minh's regime – an outcome which would be disastrous for the US policy of Communist containment.

Despite pressure from a number of advisers, President Kennedy was reluctant to become directly involved in a Vietnamese war. Instead, he chose to increase the number of 'military advisers' in the country to over 16,000, and having failed to convince Diem of the necessity for governmental reforms, he lent his tacit support to a *coup d'état* by South Vietnamese forces. If everything went according to plan, Diem would be paid-off with $1 million, provided by the CIA, and flown to a secret location outside Vietnam.

The scheme backfired spectacularly. On 2 November 1963, President Diem, along with his brother, were assassinated by their captors as they made their way into exile. The one million CIA-funded dollars disappeared. Kennedy was appalled by the outcome. Reminiscent of his reaction to the Bay of Pigs fiasco, he reportedly 'rushed from the room, with a look of shock and dismay on his face' upon hearing the news of the South Vietnamese President's brutal assassination.

Farewell to Camelot

Three weeks later, on 21 November 1963, President Kennedy, accompanied by the First Lady, travelled to Texas, where he was scheduled to make a number of appearances in a bid to drum up support for the Democratic Party prior to the 1964 general election.

Not everyone, however, was convinced of the wisdom of such a journey. Some White House officials, worried that the President would receive a hostile reception from voters in what was a staunchly Republican State, advised against it. But characteristically, Kennedy rebuffed their concerns, insisting that a trip to 'nut country' was necessary. He reportedly said to Jackie: 'if somebody wants to shoot me, […] nobody can stop it, so why worry about it?'

The following day, 22 November 1963, at 12.30pm, President Kennedy was travelling in an open top car through the streets of Dallas when three loud rifle shots rang through the air, apparently shot from the sixth floor of the nearby Book Depository building. According to official reports, the first of these bullets missed its mark, while the second penetrated the back of the President's neck. Kennedy's steel-boned back brace, which he wore to alleviate his constant pain, held Kennedy in a upright position, despite his wound – allowing the final, fatal shot to strike the back of his head.

In the ensuing chaos, the presidential limousine sped to nearby Parkland Memorial Hospital, where surgeons tried in vain to save Kennedy's life – in all probability, the impact of the third bullet had killed him instantly. At 1pm local time the 35th President of the United States was pronounced dead. He was forty-six years old.

Less than two hours later, on the tarmac of Dallas Love Field airport, Lyndon Baines Johnson was sworn in as President on board Air Force One. Standing by his side was the former First Lady, a crimson-red bloodstain despoiling her stylish pink suit.

The fairytale of Camelot was over.

Epilogue

A little over an hour after the shooting of President Kennedy, Lee Harvey Oswald – a disaffected former US Marine who had once tried, unsuccessfully, to defect to Soviet Union – was arrested on suspicion of Kennedy's murder.

Unfortunately, he was not given an opportunity to defend himself against the allegations levelled against him – two days later, as President Kennedy's body lay in State in the Capitol Rotunda in Washington DC, Oswald was shot by nightclub owner, Jack Ruby, while in police custody.

Almost immediately, various conspiracy theories began to surface. Among the most popular were allegations that Oswald was not in fact a 'lone gunman', that he was merely a pawn in a sordid assassination plot, masterminded by FBI boss, J Edgar Hoover. Another conjecture, which gained traction at the time, cast Fidel Castro as the villain of the piece, accusing him of murdering Kennedy in revenge for a rumoured CIA-backed attempt on his life.

However, while no definitive proof has ever emerged to support these hypotheses, neither have they been irrefutably disproven, despite various governmental inquiries into the assassination – most notably the Warren Commission, established by President Johnson a few days after Kennedy's funeral. Consequently much like the fascinating circumstances of his extraordinary life, the controversies surrounding John Fitzgerald Kennedy's untimely death continue to fascinate even now, almost fifty years later.

Appendix One: Key Players

Joseph Patrick Kennedy 1888–1969

Joseph Patrick Kennedy was born on Boston, Massachusetts on 6 September 1888. He was the eldest child and only surviving son of prominent businessman and politician PJ Kennedy and his wife, Mary Hickey. Having received his early education at the Catholic Xaverian School, Joe transferred to the prestigious Boston Latin School at the age of thirteen. In 1908, he was accepted to Harvard and graduated in 1912.

Highly ambitious from an early age, Joe began his career at the Columbia Trust Company, a banking institution which was controlled by his father. The young man's exceptional business acumen saw him rise quickly up the ranks, and, by the age of twenty-five, he was the country's youngest-ever bank president.

In October 1914, Joe married his long-time sweetheart, Rose Fitzgerald. The couple would go on to have nine children: four boys and five girls.

During World War One, Joe worked as an assistant manager at a major shipyard, supervising the production of warships and other equipment critical to the war effort. He later branched out into stock market trading, and avoided catastrophe by cashing in his investments before the Wall Street Crash of 1929. Having succeeded in his stated aim of becoming a millionaire by the time he was thirty-five, Kennedy's later business ventures, which included whiskey importation and movie production, only added to his fortune.

Joe first became involved in politics when he lent his support to Franklin D Roosevelt's successful presidential campaign in 1932. In exchange for his significant financial donations, Roosevelt appointed Kennedy, President of the US Securities and Exchange Commission (SEC), a newly established body tasked with regulating the financial industry. When asked to explain his decision, FDR reportedly claimed that 'it takes a thief to catch a thief', a reference to some of Joe's allegedly illegitimate business dealings.

Kennedy's tenure at the SEC was followed by a brief stint as Chairman of the Maritime Commission, and then in 1938 he was appointed as the United States Ambassador to Great Britain. However, his opposition to US intervention in World War Two made him unpopular with many senior British politicians, including Churchill. He was forced to resign in December 1940 after he declared in a newspaper interview that 'democracy is finished in England.'

In 1941, Kennedy, on the advice of doctors, authorized a lobotomy on his third child and eldest daughter, Rosemary. The twenty-three-year-old was believed to suffer from mental retardation and was prone to severe mood swings. It was hoped the procedure would alleviate her symptoms. It did not. Rosemary was left with a permanent mental disability and was institutionalized for the rest of her life. She died in 2005 at the age of eighty-six.

Joe Kennedy never made any secret of the ambitions he held for his family. 'I got Jack into politics', he told a reporter in 1957, 'I was the one. I told him Joe was dead and that it was therefore his responsibility to run for Congress. He didn't want to do it. He felt he didn't have the ability and he still feels that way. But I told him he had to do it.'

Joe Kennedy suffered from a stroke on 19 December 1961, which left him partially paralysed and without speech. Further strokes followed, and he eventually died on 18 November 1969, at the age of eighty-one. He nevertheless outlived his sons Jack and Bobby, both of whom were assassinated.

Rose Fitzgerald Kennedy 1890–1995

Born on 22 July 1890, Rose Fitzgerald was the eldest child of John Francis 'Honey Fitz' Fitzgerald and Mary Josephine Hannon. Having received her education at Dorchester High School, she graduated in 1906. An accomplished musician, Rose also studied piano at the New England Conservatory. In 1914, at the age of twenty-four, she married the ambitious Joseph Kennedy. Over the course of seventeen years, she would bear a total of nine children, only five of whom would outlive her.

A devout Roman Catholic who did not believe in divorce, Rose endured her husband's many infidelities. In 1951, Pope Pius XII bestowed on her the honorary title of 'Papal countess' in acknowledgement of her 'exemplary motherhood and many charitable works'. As she had once asked, 'Wasn't there a book about Michelangelo called *The Agony and the Ecstasy*? That's what my life has been.' Rose Fitzgerald Kennedy died on 22 January 1995, at the age of 104.

Jacqueline Lee Bouvier Kennedy Onassis 1929–1994

Born on 28 July 1929 in Southampton, New York, Jacqueline Lee Bouvier was the eldest of two daughters. Her parents were John 'Black Jack' Bouvier, a successful Wall Street stockbroker and Janet Norton Lee. The couple divorced in 1940, when Jacqueline was ten years old.

A bright child, Jacqueline enjoyed reading and did well at school. One of her teachers described her as 'a darling child, the prettiest little girl, very clever, very artistic, and full of the devil.' In addition to taking lessons in French and ballet, Jacqueline was also an accomplished equestrienne and her love of horses would last her a lifetime. Jacqueline's teenage years were spent at an exclusive boarding school in Connecticut. Graduating in 1947, she continued her education at Vassar College, where she read French, history, art, and literature. Two years later, in 1949, Jacqueline participated in a study abroad programme, which saw her relocating to France to attend the University of Grenoble and the Sorbonne. Returning to the US in 1950, she completed her education at the George Washington University in Washington DC.

She began her career in 1951 as the 'Inquiring Camera Girl' for the *Washington Times-Herald* newspaper. During this time, she was briefly engaged to John Husted, another stockbroker, but she ended the relationship in March 1952. In May of that year, Jacqueline met Senator John Fitzgerald Kennedy at a dinner party. After a 'spasmodic' courtship, they became engaged the following year. The wedding took place on 12 September 1953 at St Mary's Church in Newport, Rhode Island.

The marriage was fraught with difficulties from the outset, not least of which was Senator Kennedy's serial infidelity. Jackie's first pregnancy ended in miscarriage in 1955, and she gave birth to a stillborn daughter in August 1956. Happily, a healthy daughter, Caroline, arrived in November 1957, followed by a son, John Jr, in 1960. A second son, Patrick Bouvier Kennedy, was born on 7 August 1963, but died two days later from a respiratory illness.

Jacqueline, who disliked the shortening of her name to 'Jackie', occupied the role of First Lady of the United States from 1961 until her husband's assassination in late 1963. During this time, she dedicated herself to the restoration of the White House, and with the help of conservation specialists and art experts she succeeded in establishing the White House as the nation's cultural centre. She enjoyed widespread popularity as First Lady and was regarded as a style icon the world over.

On 22 November 1963, as she was travelling alongside her husband in an open-top car through the streets of Dallas, President Kennedy was shot. Accompanying her husband's body back to Washington DC on board Air Force One, the former First Lady witnessed the swearing in of Lyndon B Johnson as her husband's successor. Her blood-stained, pink Chanel suit became another defining image of that terrible day.

In 1968, Jacqueline married the Greek shipping tycoon, Aristotle Onassis. The pair remained together until Onassis's death in 1975. In later years, Jacqueline worked as an editor for the publishing houses Viking Press and Doubleday. She died from non-Hodgkin's lymphoma on 19 May 1994, at the age of sixty-four. She was laid to rest beside President Kennedy in the Arlington National Cemetery in Virginia.

Lyndon B Johnson 1908–1973

Often referred to simply as 'LBJ', Lyndon Baines Johnson was born on 27 August 1908 in Stonewall, Texas, where his family owned a small farmstead. He was the eldest child of Sam Ealy Johnson and his wife Rebekah Baines. In 1913, the family moved to Johnson City, which was named after LBJ's ancestors, who had helped to settle the area. Here, he attended the Johnson City High School, graduating in 1924. In 1927, Johnson enrolled at the Southwest Texas State Teachers College, earning a Bachelor of Science in 1930.

Moving to Washington in 1931, Johnson worked as secretary

to Congressman Richard Kleberg. By 1934, he had met Claudia 'Lady Bird' Alta Taylor, and the pair married in November of that year. The couple went on to have two children, Lynda and Luci.

In 1937, Johnson was elected to the House of Representatives as Congressman for the 10th Congressional District of Texas. After six terms in Congress, he successfully ran for the Senate in 1948 and, in 1953, became the youngest-ever Minority Leader. In 1960, LBJ won the Democratic Party's vice-presidential nomination and contested the general election alongside the presidential nominee, John Fitzgerald Kennedy.

On 8 November, the Kennedy–Johnson ticket narrowly defeated their rivals. Both men were sworn into office on 20 January 1961. Less than three years later, on 22 November 1963, Johnson became the 36th President of the United States, following Kennedy's assassination in Dallas. He took his Oath of Office on Air Force One, in the presence of Jackie Kennedy, who was accompanying her husband's body back to Washington. LBJ was re-elected in the 1964 presidential election.

One of his first acts as President was to establish 'The President's Commission on the Assassination of President Kennedy' (otherwise known as the Warren Commission). During his time in office, Johnson signed into law Kennedy's Civil Rights Bill. He also introduced major reforms to social services, approving federal funding for education, and establishing the Medicare and Medicaid programmes. However, his decision to reverse Kennedy's planned withdrawal of troops from Vietnam was criticized in some quarters, and his popularity suffered greatly as opposition to the Vietnam War mounted.

Worried about his failing health and struggling to cope with the internal party tensions caused by the ongoing war in Vietnam, LBJ shocked the nation by announcing in March 1968, that he would not be contesting the presidential election later that year. Upon leaving the White House, LBJ and Lady Bird retired to their ranch in Texas. He died of heart failure four years later, on 22 January 1973. He was sixty-four years old.

Robert Kennedy 1925–1968

Robert Francis 'Bobby' Kennedy was born on 20 November 1925, the seventh child of Joe Sr and Rose Kennedy. He was educated at Milton Academy, a preparatory school in Massachusetts. Kennedy was accepted to Harvard in 1946. After graduating with a degree in Government, he continued his studies at the University of Virginia, gaining a law degree in 1951. A year earlier, Bobby had married Ethel Skakel, with whom he would have eleven children.

Kennedy began working at the Department of Justice in 1951, but left a year later to manage his brother's successful Senate campaign. He later worked for Senator McCarthy on his controversial Subcommittee on Investigations. Controversially, Bobby was appointed Attorney General by President Kennedy in 1961. Following his brother's assassination, Kennedy launched a successful bid for a seat in the Senate, and four years later, he announced his intention to run for president.

Robert Kennedy was shot on 5 June 1968, at the Ambassador Hotel in California, shortly after winning the Californian Democratic primary. He died the following day and was buried at Arlington National Cemetery in Virginia.

Lee Harvey Oswald 1939–1963

Lee Harvey Oswald was born two months after his father's death on 18 October 1939 in New Orleans. A troublesome student,

Oswald was referred to a psychiatrist in his early teens. He was diagnosed with a 'personality disorder', now thought to have been schizophrenia, but did not receive any treatment. In 1956, he joined the US Marines, where he became a skilled marksman. Oswald, however, harboured Communist sympathies and, in 1959 he left the United States for the Soviet Union.

In 1961, after a six-week courtship, Oswald married Marina Nikolayevna Prusakova in Minsk. The couple's first child was born in February 1962. Having been unsuccessful in his bid to gain Soviet citizenship, the family returned to the US in June.

In October 1963, just before the birth of his second daughter, Oswald started work at the Texas Book Depository in Dallas. Six weeks later, he allegedly smuggled his rifle into the building and shot President Kennedy from a sixth floor window. Forty-five minutes after the assassination, Oswald allegedly shot a policeman before being arrested a little time later while taking refuge in a movie theatre. Oswald was shot in the abdomen by Jack Ruby on 24 November 1963 as authorities were preparing to transfer him to county jail. He died at around 1pm at Parkland Memorial Hospital.

Jack Ruby 1911–1967

Jack Ruby was born Jacob Rubenstein on 25 March 1911, in Chicago, Illinois. The son of Polish émigrés, he was the fifth of eight surviving children. Jack had a difficult childhood, and spent some time in care at foster homes.

In 1943, Ruby was drafted into the United States Air Army Forces and was honourably discharged in 1946, after which time he became involved in the nightclub business. He was also rumoured to have been involved in organized crime.

On 24 November 1963, Ruby shot Lee Harvey Oswald in the abdomen as authorities were preparing to transfer Oswald to county jail. The assassination was captured by a number of television cameras and was broadcast live to the nation. On 14 March 1964, Ruby was found guilty of the Oswald's murder and sentenced to death. Ruby appealed both the conviction and the sentence, but died of lung cancer on 3 January 1967, before his appeal came to court.

Nikita Khrushchev 1894–1971

Nikita Sergeyevich Khrushchev was born in April 1894 into a poor mining family near the current Ukrainian–Russian border. As a child, he received little schooling, and worked from a young age to help support the family.

He signed up to the Bolshevik Party in 1918, and fought for the Red Army in the Russian Civil War. By 1929, he enrolled in the Stalin Industrial Academy, and two years later, he had gained employment within the Communist Party. He advanced quickly and became a member of the Politburo in 1939. He was soon despatched to Ukraine, where he carried on Stalin's campaign of political suppression. His actions in support of Stalin's purges earned him the nickname 'the butcher of the Ukraine'.

Khrushchev became First Secretary of the Communist Party following Stalin's death in 1953, and Premier of the Soviet Union in 1958. However, his mishandling of relations with the West during the Cold War, including his questionable decision-making during the Cuban Missile Crisis, made him unpopular and he was eventually ousted in 1964. He died on 11 September 1971.

Appendix Two: Timeline of JFK

1917
29 May: John Fitzgerald Kennedy was born in Brookline, Massachusetts

1931
September: Enrols at Choate School, an Episcopalian institution in Connecticut

1935
June: Graduates from Choate, 65th out of a class of 110
September: Travels to London with the intention of studying for a year at LSE, but health problems force him to abandon his plans
October: Enrols at Princeton University, but soon drops out

1936
September: Begins his undergraduate career at Harvard University

1938
Winter: Takes a break from Harvard and embarks on an extended European tour

1939
September: Outbreak of World War Two; Kennedy leaves Europe and returns to America

1940

June: Graduates from Harvard University with a degree in International Affairs

July: Kennedy's Harvard thesis is published as a book called *Why England Slept*

1941

October: Kennedy joins the US Navy

7 December: Japanese bomb Pearl Harbour and America enters World War Two

1943

March: Kennedy assumes command of PT-109 and deploys to the Solomon Islands

2 August: PT-109 is sunk by a Japanese destroyer. Kennedy and surviving crew are stranded behind enemy lines; they are rescued six days later

1944

11 June: Kennedy receives the Navy and Corps Medal for bravery

12 August: Kennedy's older brother, Joe Jr, is killed in action

1945

1 March: Discharged from the navy on medical grounds

1946

25 April: Formally announces his intention to run for Congress

18 June: Wins the Democratic congressional nomination for the 11th District of Massachusetts

5 November: Elected to the US House of Representatives

1947

September: Diagnosed as having Addison's Disease

1948

2 November: Re-elected to the House of Representatives, unopposed

1950

7 November: Re-elected to the House of Representatives, winning over 82 per cent of the vote

1952

24 April: Announces his intention to run for the US Senate
10 May: Encounters Jacqueline Lee Bouvier at a dinner party
4 November: Elected as Senator for Massachusetts

1953

24 June: Jack and Jackie's engagement is officially announced
12 September: The couple marry in Newport, Rhode Island

1954

21 October: Kennedy undergoes surgery in an attempt to alleviate chronic back pain
2 December: Kennedy abstains from Senate vote to censure Senator Joe McCarthy

1955

February: Undergoes the second back surgery. While recuperating, he writes his second book, *Profiles in Courage*

1956

17 August: Narrowly loses the Democratic vice presidential nomination at the Party's Chicago convention

23 August: Jackie gives birth to a stillborn daughter. Kennedy is reluctant to cut short his vacation to be by his wife's side

1957

6 May: *Profiles in Courage* wins the Pulitzer Prize for Biography
27 November: Kennedy's first surviving child, Caroline, is born

1958

4 November: Kennedy is re-elected to the Senate

1960

2 January: Kennedy officially declares his candidature for the Presidency of the United States
15 July: Kennedy wins the Democratic primary
8 November: Americans go to the polls in vast numbers
9 November: Nixon concedes JFK is declared the country's 35th President
25 November: John Fitzgerald Kennedy Jr, the couple's second surviving child, is born

1961

20 January: Kennedy is sworn in to office, giving an inspiring inaugural address
1 March: Kennedy establishes the Peace Corps
17–19 April: The Bay of Pigs mission is launched and ends in defeat
3–4 June: Kennedy meets Nikita Khrushchev in Vienna
13 August: Construction begins on the Berlin Wall

1962

14–28 October: Cuban Missile Crisis

1963

11 June: President Kennedy orders the Governor of Alabama to allow the registration of black students at the University of Alabama. Announces his intention to introduce Civil Rights legislation to Congress

5 August: American and the Soviet Union agree terms for a Partial Nuclear Test Ban Treaty

7 August: Jackie gives birth to the couple's second son, Patrick Bouvier Kennedy

9 August: Patrick Kennedy dies as a result of respiratory problems

21 November: President and Mrs Kennedy travel to Texas

22 November: President Kennedy is assassinated by Lee Harvey Oswald in Dealey Plaza, Dallas at 12.30pm. His death is confirmed by doctors at 1pm. Lyndon B Johnson is sworn in as President of the United States at 2.38pm

24 November: Oswald is shot by Jack Ruby while in police custody

25 November: Following a service at St Matthew's Cathedral, Kennedy is laid to rest at Arlington National Cemetery in Virginia

29 November: President Johnson established the Warren Commission to investigate Kennedy's assassination

1964

29 September: The Warren Commission publishes its report; it finds no evidence of conspiracy

Got Another Hour?

History in an Hour is a series of eBooks to help the reader learn the basic facts of a given subject area. Everything you need to know is presented in a straightforward narrative and in chronological order. No embedded links to divert your attention, nor a daunting book of 600 pages with a 35-page introduction. Just straight in, to the point, sixty minutes, done. Then, having absorbed the basics, you may feel inspired to explore further. Give yourself sixty minutes and see what you can learn…

To find out more visit http://historyinanhour.com or follow us on twitter: http://twitter.com/historyinanhour

1066: History in an Hour by Kaye Jones

Covering the major events of the year 1066, this is a clear account of England's political turmoil during which the country had three different kings and fought three large-scale battles in defence of the kingdom, including the infamous Battle of Hastings.

The Afghan Wars: History in an Hour by Rupert Colley

A comprehensive overview of the wars that have been fought in Afghanistan for almost four decades, including the politics of the Taliban, why Osama Bin Laden was so significant, and why it is still so hard to achieve peace in the country.

The American Civil War: History in an Hour by Kat Smutz

A clear account of the politics and major turning points of the war that split the country in half as the northern and southern states fought over the right to keep slaves, changing American culture forever.

American Slavery: History in an Hour by Kat Smutz

A broad overview of the major events in the history of American slavery, detailing the arrival of the first slaves, the Southern plantations, the Civil War, and the historical and cultural legacy of slavery in the United States.

Ancient Egypt: History in an Hour by Anthony Holmes

A succinct exploration of the historic rise of Egyptian civilisation and its influence on the world, covering Egyptian gods, mummification and burial rituals, and the Pyramids of Giza.

Black History: History in an Hour by Rupert Colley

A clear overview of the long and varied history of African Americans, including everything from slavery, the Civil War and emancipation to the civil rights movement and the Black Panther Party.

The Cold War: History in an Hour by Rupert Colley

A succinct overview of the politics of the non-violent war, from the end of World War II to the collapse of the USSR in 1991, as Russia and America eyed each other with suspicion and hostility.

Dickens: History in an Hour by Kaye Jones

A comprehensive overview of the life of arguably Britain's most successful and beloved writer, including the poverty of his childhood, the evolution of his novels, his tours of Europe and America, and his occasionally scandalous private life.

George Washington: History in an Hour by David B. McCoy

The essential chronicle of George Washington's life, from his middle-class Virginian upbringing to his unanimous election as America's first president, and the prominent role he played in shaping America as we know it today.

The Gunpowder Plot: History in an Hour by Sinead Fitzgibbon

An engaging account of the infamous plot by a group of Catholic traitors, led by Guy Fawkes, to blow up the Houses of Parliament and James I, including details of the motives behind their drastic actions and how the plot came to be discovered.

Henry VIII's Wives: History in an Hour by Julie Wheeler

An inclusive introduction to the six diverse personalities of Henry VIII's wives, the events that led them to their individual fates, and the different impacts they each had on King and country.

Hitler: History in an Hour by Rupert Colley

A coherent overview of Hitler's early life, service in World War I, rise to the top of the Nazi Party and eventually the head of state, covering all the key moments of the dictator's life through to his death and the crumbling of his empire.

The Medieval Anarchy: History in an Hour by Kaye Jones

A look at the unprecedented chaos and disorder that followed the death of King Henry I, leading to England's first, and often forgotten, civil war, as well as an overview of the plots and violence that ensued during this nineteen-year bloody conflict.

Nazi Germany: History in an Hour by Rupert Colley

A concise explanation which covers the major events behind the Nazi Party's climb to power, what it was like to live in Nazi Germany, and how Hitler brought the world into war.

The Queen: History in an Hour by Sinead Fitzgibbon

A compelling history of the UK's second-longest-reigning monarch, covering her 1953 coronation to her Diamond Jubilee in 2012 and examining her long reign, during which the British Empire has transformed.

The Reformation: History in an Hour by Edward A. Gosselin

A concise look at the spread of religious dissidence across Europe in the sixteenth century, including the events that caused people to question the ideas of the established Catholic Church and the resulting wars, migration and disunity.

The Russian Revolution: History in an Hour by Rupert Colley

Covering all the major events in a straightforward overview of the greatest political experiment ever conducted, and how it continues to influence both Eastern and Western politics today.

The Siege of Leningrad: History in an Hour by Rupert Colley

A broad account of one of the longest sieges in history in which over the course of 900 days the city of Leningrad resisted German invasion, contributing to the defeat of the Nazis at the cost of over one million civilian lives.

South Africa: History in an Hour by Anthony Holmes

A fascinating overview of South Africa's history of oppression and racial inequality and how after years of violence and apartheid, Nelson Mandela, the country's first black President, led the country to unite and become the 'Rainbow Nation'.

Stalin: History in an Hour by Rupert Colley

A succinct exploration of Joseph Stalin's long leadership of the Soviet Union, covering his rise to power, his role in the Russian Revolution, and his terrifying regime that directly and negatively affected the lives of so many.

Titanic: History in an Hour by Sinead Fitzgibbon

An account of the catastrophe, including the failures of the White Star Line, the significance of class and the legacy of the disaster in Britain and America.

The Vietnam War: History in an Hour by Neil Smith

A clear account of the key events of the most important Cold War-era conflict, including the circumstances leading up to the Vietnam War, the deadly guerrilla warfare, the fall of Saigon and the backlash of anti-war protests in America.

World War One: History in an Hour by Rupert Colley

A clear overview of the road to war, the major turning points and battles, and the key leaders involved, as well as the lasting impact the Great War had on almost every country in the world.

World War Two: History in an Hour by Rupert Colley

Covering the major events in a broad overview of the politics and violence of the most devastating conflict the world has ever seen, and how it changed the world in unimaginable ways.